When people travel with camels, the animals usually walk in a single file. Some of the camels carry loads and others carry people. This is called a *caravan*. In the past, some caravans contained thousands of camels. But today, they are usually much smaller than that, like the one shown below.

During the Middle Ages, most of the spices that were sent from the Far East to Europe traveled part of the way on the backs of camels. Huge caravans carried the spices and other valuable goods across Arabia. And camels became famous throughout the known world as pack animals. In fact, the name *camel* may come from the work that camels have done as pack animals. It may come from the ancient Middle Eastern word *gamel*, which means "carrying a burden."

Since camels are also used as riding animals, they are often described with the same terms that are used for horses. A male camel is called a *stallion*. A female is a *mare*, and a young camel is called a *foal*. Male and female camels look very much alike, although males are usually a little larger. All members of the camel family have long necks, woolly coats, and thin legs.

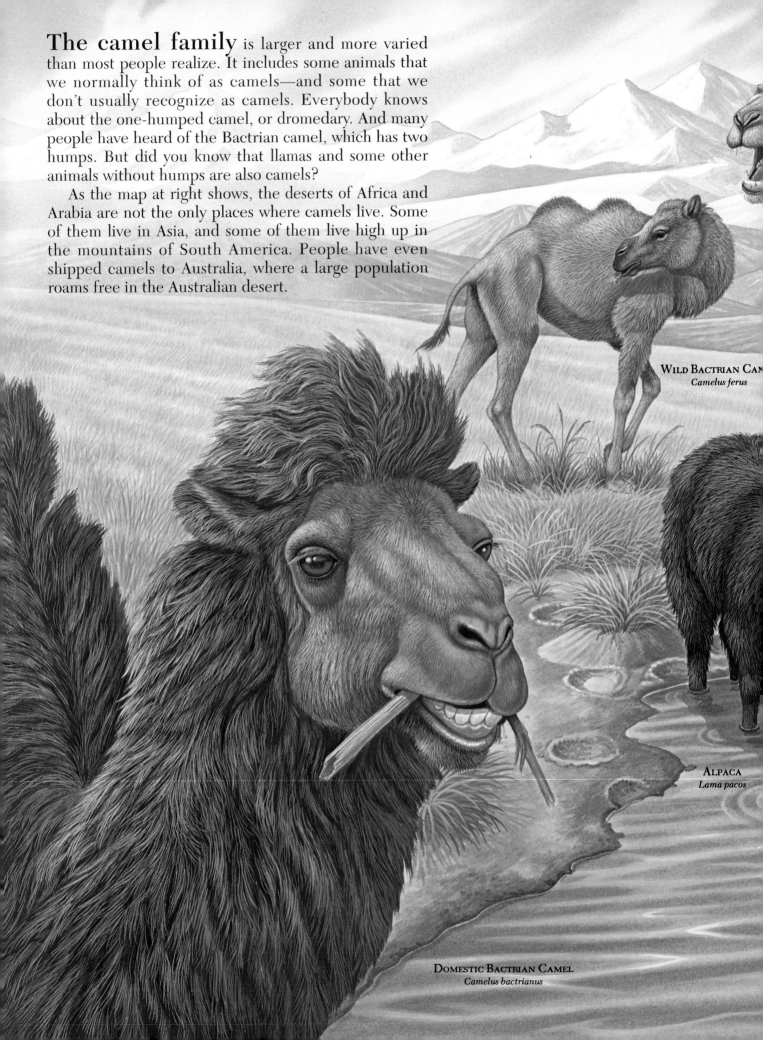

The camel family is larger and more varied than most people realize. It includes some animals that we normally think of as camels—and some that we don't usually recognize as camels. Everybody knows about the one-humped camel, or dromedary. And many people have heard of the Bactrian camel, which has two humps. But did you know that llamas and some other animals without humps are also camels?

As the map at right shows, the deserts of Africa and Arabia are not the only places where camels live. Some of them live in Asia, and some of them live high up in the mountains of South America. People have even shipped camels to Australia, where a large population roams free in the Australian desert.

WILD BACTRIAN CAM
Camelus ferus

ALPACA
Lama pacos

DOMESTIC BACTRIAN CAMEL
Camelus bactrianus

DROMEDARY
Camelus dromedarius

DROMEDARY CAMELS
SOUTH AMERICAN CAMELS
BACTRIAN CAMELS

VICUNA
Vicugna vicugna

GUANACO
Lama guanicoe

LLAMA
Lama glama

3

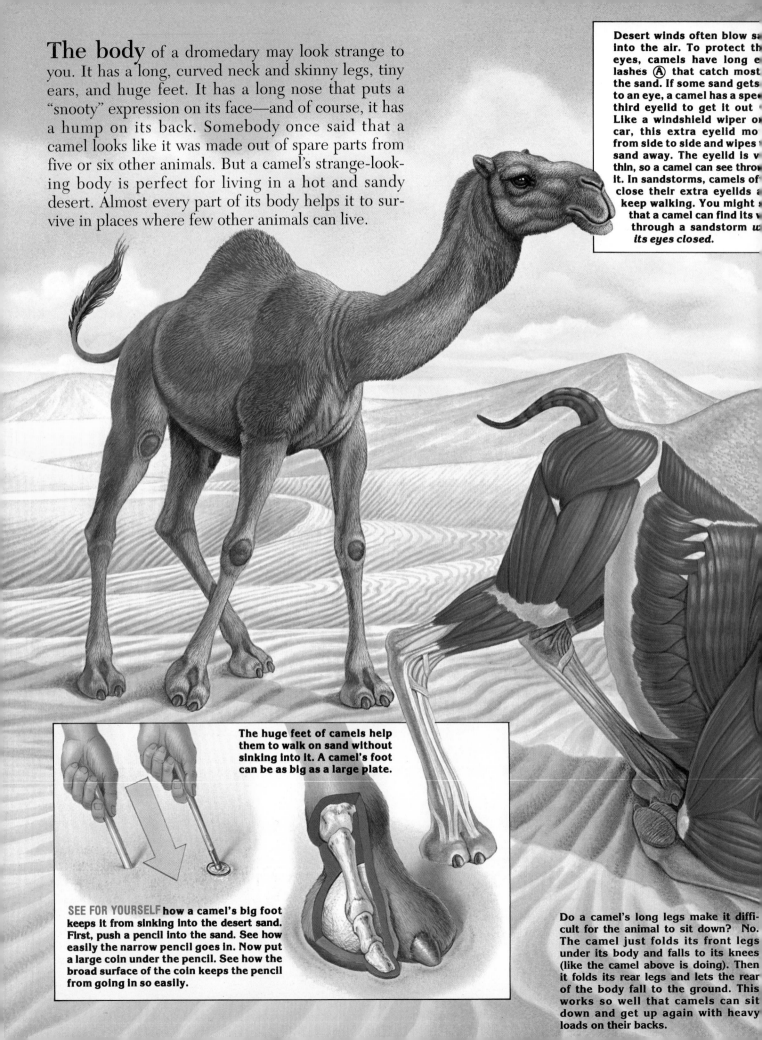

The body of a dromedary may look strange to you. It has a long, curved neck and skinny legs, tiny ears, and huge feet. It has a long nose that puts a "snooty" expression on its face—and of course, it has a hump on its back. Somebody once said that a camel looks like it was made out of spare parts from five or six other animals. But a camel's strange-looking body is perfect for living in a hot and sandy desert. Almost every part of its body helps it to survive in places where few other animals can live.

Desert winds often blow sa into the air. To protect th eyes, camels have long e lashes Ⓐ that catch most the sand. If some sand gets to an eye, a camel has a spe third eyelid to get it out Like a windshield wiper or car, this extra eyelid mo from side to side and wipes sand away. The eyelid is v thin, so a camel can see throu it. In sandstorms, camels of close their extra eyelids a keep walking. You might that a camel can find its through a sandstorm w *its eyes closed.*

The huge feet of camels help them to walk on sand without sinking into it. A camel's foot can be as big as a large plate.

SEE FOR YOURSELF how a camel's big foot keeps it from sinking into the desert sand. First, push a pencil into the sand. See how easily the narrow pencil goes in. Now put a large coin under the pencil. See how the broad surface of the coin keeps the pencil from going in so easily.

Do a camel's long legs make it difficult for the animal to sit down? No. The camel just folds its front legs under its body and falls to its knees (like the camel above is doing). Then it folds its rear legs and lets the rear of the body fall to the ground. This works so well that camels can sit down and get up again with heavy loads on their backs.

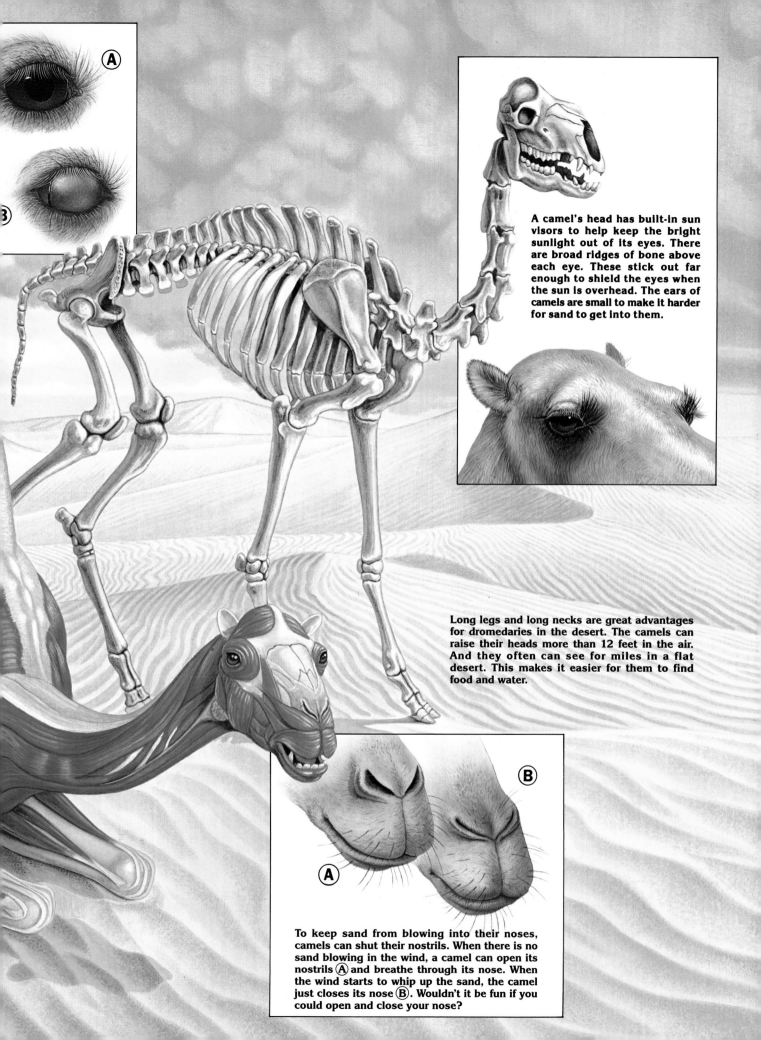

A camel's head has built-in sun visors to help keep the bright sunlight out of its eyes. There are broad ridges of bone above each eye. These stick out far enough to shield the eyes when the sun is overhead. The ears of camels are small to make it harder for sand to get into them.

Long legs and long necks are great advantages for dromedaries in the desert. The camels can raise their heads more than 12 feet in the air. And they often can see for miles in a flat desert. This makes it easier for them to find food and water.

To keep sand from blowing into their noses, camels can shut their nostrils. When there is no sand blowing in the wind, a camel can open its nostrils Ⓐ and breathe through its nose. When the wind starts to whip up the sand, the camel just closes its nose Ⓑ. Wouldn't it be fun if you could open and close your nose?

Camels don't need to drink water

as often as other animals because they can *conserve* water better than most other animals can. A camel doesn't carry an extra supply of water in its hump, as many people believe. Instead, it has a number of ways to limit the amount of water its body uses, and so *it doesn't need* an extra supply.

Most animals sweat a lot in the desert, and use up the water in their bodies very fast. But camels have ways to keep from sweating too much. And they can also stay alive with less water in their bodies than other animals can. With camels, a little water goes a long way.

In the hottest part of the desert, during the hottest time of the year, a camel can go for a week or more without taking a drink. And during the cooler winter months, camels sometimes go for *six months* without drinking.

Camels lose water from their bodies very slowly—and they can lose an incredibly large amount of water and still stay alive. These are the main reasons why camels can outlast people and other animals in the desert. See what happens when a man, a cow, a donkey and a camel take a trip together in the desert when the weather is fairly hot.

The hump is really a place for storing *fat* instead of water. Like the fat on people, camel fat is a source of energy.

When a camel goes without water for some time, its body starts to dry out. The body gets smaller and the ribs begin to show. When a camel is really dry, a hollow area can be seen behind the ribs. People who own camels can often tell how much water a camel needs by the size of the hollow spot. Can you find it on the thirsty camel at right?

When camels finally do drink, they may take in enormous amounts of water. When the weather is hot, some camels can drink as much as 35 gallons of water at one time. And they may guzzle all of that down in less than six minutes! A really thirsty camel may drink more than 50 gallons in one day.

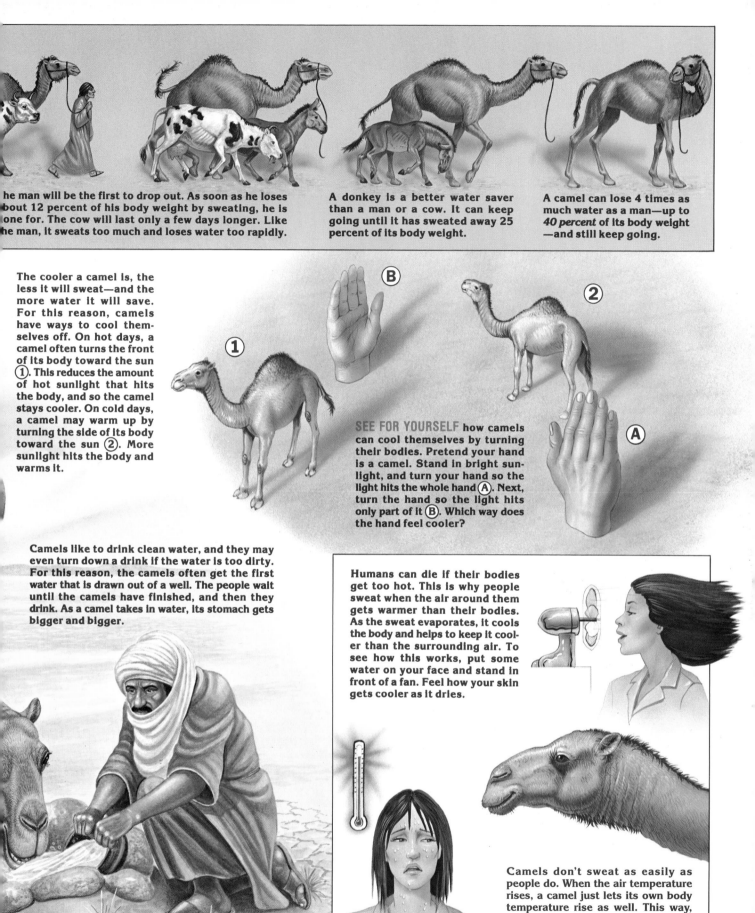

he man will be the first to drop out. As soon as he loses bout 12 percent of his body weight by sweating, he is lone for. The cow will last only a few days longer. Like he man, it sweats too much and loses water too rapidly.

A donkey is a better water saver than a man or a cow. It can keep going until it has sweated away 25 percent of its body weight.

A camel can lose 4 times as much water as a man—up to *40 percent* of its body weight —and still keep going.

The cooler a camel is, the less it will sweat—and the more water it will save. For this reason, camels have ways to cool themselves off. On hot days, a camel often turns the front of its body toward the sun ①. This reduces the amount of hot sunlight that hits the body, and so the camel stays cooler. On cold days, a camel may warm up by turning the side of its body toward the sun ②. More sunlight hits the body and warms it.

SEE FOR YOURSELF how camels can cool themselves by turning their bodies. Pretend your hand is a camel. Stand in bright sunlight, and turn your hand so the light hits the whole hand Ⓐ. Next, turn the hand so the light hits only part of it Ⓑ. Which way does the hand feel cooler?

Camels like to drink clean water, and they may even turn down a drink if the water is too dirty. For this reason, the camels often get the first water that is drawn out of a well. The people wait until the camels have finished, and then they drink. As a camel takes in water, its stomach gets bigger and bigger.

Humans can die if their bodies get too hot. This is why people sweat when the air around them gets warmer than their bodies. As the sweat evaporates, it cools the body and helps to keep it cooler than the surrounding air. To see how this works, put some water on your face and stand in front of a fan. Feel how your skin gets cooler as it dries.

Camels don't sweat as easily as people do. When the air temperature rises, a camel just lets its own body temperature rise as well. This way, the camel doesn't start to sweat until the air gets really hot—and this saves a lot of water. A camel can let its body temperature rise six degrees Fahrenheit without hurting itself.

People and camels need each other in the harsh world of the desert. In fact, if the people did not have camels, they would not be able to survive. And if the camels did not have people, they would not survive.

Most of the water in the desert is found at the bottom of deep wells, where camels cannot get to it. The camels need people to draw the water up for them. They work for people in order to get water.

The people of the desert need camels to carry them from place to place, and for other reasons as well. Most of the people are *nomads*. They live in tents and wander across the desert, stopping wherever they find food and water. Without camels, it would be impossible for them to do this.

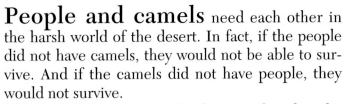

Camels don't really carry other camels on their backs. But we wanted to show you that some of them are strong enough to carry a load that weighs as much as they do. This strength is the main reason why nomads depend so much on camels. Camels are the *only* animals that can live in the desert and carry heavy loads from place to place.

CAMELS ACTIVITIES

by Carol Spirkoff Prime

A SHADY CHARACTER

To make this wild and shady character, you will need to shade some of the squares in the grid below. You will use these five patterns: ▨ ▨ ◸ ◹ ◼. Use the information in the orange box to figure out which squares to shade and which patterns to use.

For example, you will color the square for **D9** with the ◣ pattern. To find the square for **D9**, look for the **D** across the top of the grid. Then, look for the **9** down the side of the grid. Now, find the square where the **D** and the **9** meet. Use pencil to shade it like this ◣.

◣ **D9, E12, F13, L9, N10, O11**

◢ **A10, B5, C4, D3, E2, F1, J1, O12, R4, S1**

◤ **F12, H1, L1, M2, N3, N9, O4, O10, P11, T1, W2**

◥ **B10, C9, F9, N8, O13, P12, R7, S6, T5, U4, V3**

◼ **A11, A12, A13, B9, C5, D4, D5, D6, D7, D8, E7, F2, F7, F8, G1, G2, G7, G8, H2, H7, I2, I7, J2, J3, J4, J5, J6, J7, J8, K1, K2, L2, M9, M10, M11, N4, N5, N6, N7, R5, R6, S2, S3, S4, S5, T4, V2**

SAVE THE EARTH: WATER CONSERVATION

In Asia, people are taking away the precious water that the wild camels need. Worldwide people need to think about using water resources more wisely. By doing so, they are saving precious water and energy.

Here are some things you can do in your home to save water.

1. For a day, make a record of every time you use some water. Carry around a notepad. Write down how much water you use and how you use it. Later, look over your list to see what you could do to use less water.

2. Search for leaks. Look closely at pipes and faucets. Get help from an adult in your family to fix the leaks.

3. Compare the amount of water you use for taking a shower and for a bath. To do so, simply put the plug in the bathtub drain while you take a shower. Compare this to the amount of water you usually use when taking a bath.

To learn more about how the ways people use water affect camels, see pages 16 and 17. In what other ways do people affect camels?

Can you find the picture in this book of a woman weaving or desert nomad from the Middle East. (This is the striped area page 3.) After reading about what she is doing, follow these a weaving of your own.

You will need a 6 x 6 inch piece of cardboard, a ruler, a pencil, string, scissors, colored yarn.

1. Mark the top edge of the cardboard every ¼ inch. Make a small cut where each mark is. Now do the same with the bottom edge of the cardboard.

2. Tightly wind string around the cardboard, as shown. Notice that each loop of string goes into a cut in the cardboard. Tightly tie together the two ends to hold them in place (these tied ends are the back of the loom).

3. Thi
wa
Ch
tha
ya
12

4. We
ya
cardboard loom. The yarn goes **over** the **under** the next piece of string. Put it **und** remaining string on the loom.

5. The next piece of yarn goes opposite the **and under** the pieces of string on the loo

COLOR THE CAMEL

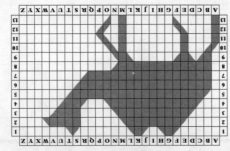

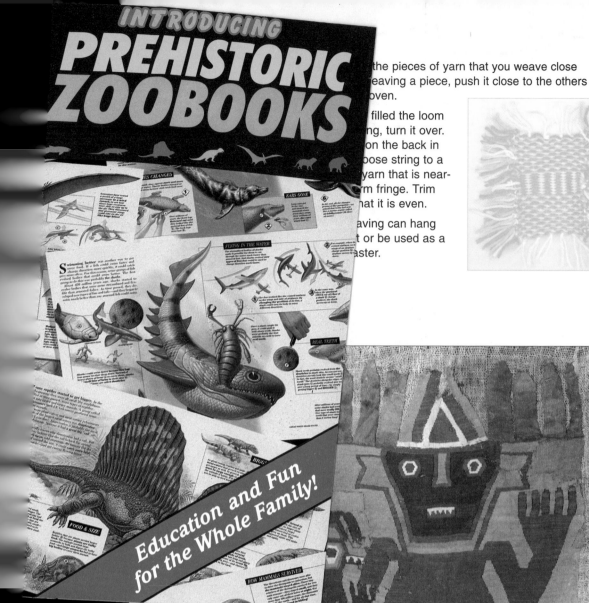

the pieces of yarn that you weave close
...eaving a piece, push it close to the others
...oven.

...filled the loom
...ng, turn it over.
...on the back in
...oose string to a
...yarn that is near-
...rm fringe. Trim
...at it is even.

...aving can hang
...t or be used as a
...aster.

...er each

...t goes **over**

People living nearly one thousand years ago wove this piece of cloth
out of the wool from a camel. The people lived in what is now Peru.
Challenge: The wool from what type of camel was used to create this
interesting work of art?

San Diego Museum of Man

Parents, try these activities with your young children:

○ With your child, read and discuss
the information about a camel's
foot in the box on page 4. Then, try
the demonstration together. Let
your child see how much resistance
the quarter creates. Ask, "Why do
camels have big feet?"

○ Focus your child's attention on the
photographs of camels transporting
people. Discuss different kinds of
transportation by asking your child
"What are some ways people use
to get from place to place?"
(Answers include cars, trucks,
trains, planes, buses, bikes, roller-
skates, horses, donkeys, and
camels, among others.) Then,
help your child cut out magazine
pictures showing different kinds
of transportation. Put the pictures
in a scrap book or make a collage.
Encourage him or her to take
photographs, or draw pictures to
add to the scrapbook.

○ Go outside with your child. Allow
him or her to put on a visor and to
describe how it shades his or her
eyes from the sun. Then, compare
a visor with the brow ridges of a
camel. Ask, "What job do both of
these do?" For more information,
see page 5. Remind your child
never to look directly at the sun.

MAKE A CAMEL COLLAGE

*You will need colored construction paper, scraps of
other kinds of paper, scissors, glue or paste, and a
black felt pen.*

Look through the pages of this book to see in what
types of environment camels live. Then, plan and
create a camel collage following these steps.

1. First, choose the environment. Cut shapes out of
paper to create the environment.

2. Then, match the right type of camel to your chosen
environment. Cut camel shapes out of paper.

3. Arrange all of the cut shapes on a large piece of
construction paper. Glue or paste the shapes in
place. Add a few details with felt pen.

Share your collage with your friends and family.

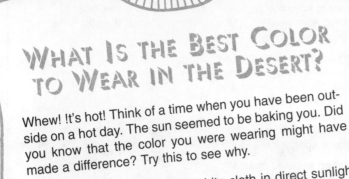

WHAT IS THE BEST COLOR TO WEAR IN THE DESERT?

Whew! It's hot! Think of a time when you have been outside on a hot day. The sun seemed to be baking you. Did you know that the color you were wearing might have made a difference? Try this to see why.

1. Place a black cloth and a white cloth in direct sunlight for 20 minutes. After 20 minutes, touch both pieces of cloth. Which feels warmer? Which would you want to wear on a hot day?

2. Can you guess what color is worn by people who ride camels in the hot desert? To find out, turn to page 1. As you probably figured out, they are wearing light colored clothes. Notice, too, that the clothes are loose fitting and cover much of the body to protect it from the sun.

3. Now, design an outfit to wear on a hot day. Sketch your ideas on paper. Your outfit can be fantastic—one that you probably wouldn't really wear. Or, it can be realistic—one that you and your friends might wear to school.

Think about what you learned next time you get dressed on a hot day. Stay cool.

CAMEL WORDS

3 LETTERS
SUN

4 LETTERS
FOAL
HUMP

5 LETTERS
DRINK
LLAMA
NOMAD

6 LETTERS
ALPACA
DESERT
VICUNA

7 LETTERS
CARAVAN
SURVIVE

8 LETTERS
STALLION

9 LETTERS
~~DROMEDARY~~

NOT A CROSS WORD ABOUT CAMELS

Place the camel words in the puzzle below so the letters fit together like a crossword. You will use each word only once. Cross each word off the list after writing it in the puzzle. The first answer is done for you. *Hint:* Notice that a new word starts at each **d** in the word *dromedary* as it is written in the puzzle. The first **d**-word has 6 letters and the second **d**-word has 5 letters.

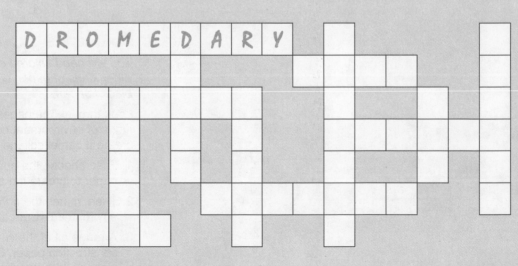

The hair of camels is used to make clothes for the nomads to wear and tents for them to live in. During the summer, some of the hair on camels falls out, and the nomads gather it. The camels grow new hair before the winter comes.

Camels even provide entertainment for the nomads. Special breeds of camels are used for racing, and camel racing is an important social event among the desert tribes. The fastest camels can run as fast as a horse for short distances. In fact, the name "dromedary" comes from an ancient Greek word that means "running."

All desert tribes depend on camel meat and milk as an important part of their food supply. Some tribes eat camel meat all the time. Others feel that their camels are too valuable for that, so they only serve camel meat on special occasions.

In many places, camels are used as money. When people buy something, they may pay with camels. And the number of camels that nomads have is a sign of how wealthy they are. Odd-shaped camels are often worth more than regular camels. A camel with four humps once sold for $10,000!

Rain storms don't happen very often in the desert. But when they do, they can cause trouble for camel owners. With so much water around, the camels don't need people anymore to get water for them. While it's raining, the camels may try to break away from their owners and run away. When the rain stops, some of the camels may come back. But some of them never do.

People and camels may need each other, but this doesn't mean that they always get along with each other. Camels can have nasty tempers. And once they decide they don't like somebody, they may carry a grudge for years. An angry camel can be dangerous, with its sharp teeth and powerful body. So smart camel owners sometimes use a clever method to calm their camels. They give the camels the coats off their backs, *and let the camels rip them to shreds.* When the camels have finished destroying their masters' coats, they often seem to feel a lot better!

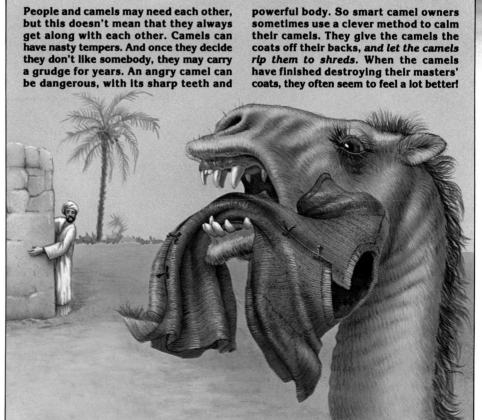

Bactrian camels have two humps. They are also shorter than dromedaries, and have heavier bodies. In general, Bactrian camels are more gentle than dromedaries. And their two humps make them easier to ride, since they form a kind of "saddle" on the animal's back.

Unlike dromedaries, Bactrian camels don't have to live in a hot and flat desert. They can survive in high mountains, where it can get very cold. In fact, most Bactrian camels live in the mountains of Asia, where dromedaries could never live. Most Bactrians live with people, like dromedaries. But there are still some wild Bactrian camels in remote areas.

It's really easy to tell if camel is a dromedary a Bactrian. The singl hump of a dromeda looks like the letter "D —the first letter in th word "dromedary."

Most Bactrian camels live in mountain deserts, like the one shown above. In these places, they survive an incredible range of hot and cold temperatures. During the summer, the temperature may climb to 122 degrees Fahrenheit. In winter, it may drop to 20 degrees below zero, and the camels may find themselves wearing caps of snow on their heads.

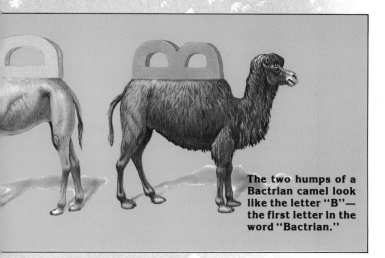

The two humps of a Bactrian camel look like the letter "B"— the first letter in the word "Bactrian."

Camels are plant-eating animals, but male camels have teeth that look like the teeth of meat-eating animals. The male's front teeth are long and sharp.

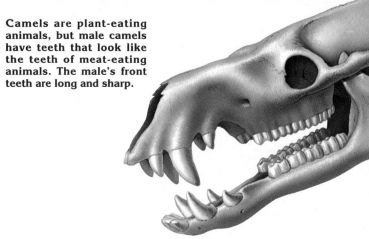

The big teeth of male camels are used when they fight other males. In a camel fight, each animal nips at the other with its teeth. And they try to force each other to the ground, as shown below. Most fighting takes place during the mating season, when the males fight over females.

Two-humped camels are called Bactrian camels because they were probably tamed for the first time in a part of Asia called Baktria, about 3,000 years ago. In ancient times, they were used in wars. The camel shown in this old sculpture was part of the army of an ancient king of Persia.

Nomads in Asia depend on Bactrian camels in many of the same ways that nomads in Africa depend on dromedaries. The camels provide wool, meat, and milk. They are used for carrying loads and for riding. Some of them are even hitched to wagons. In return for this work, the people feed and water the camels.

DOMESTIC BACTRIAN CAMEL

To keep them warm in the winter, domestic Bactrian camels have very long hair. On some parts of their bodies it may be more than 10 inches long.

Wild Bactrian camels are much thinner than domestic Bactrians, and they have shorter hair. They almost look like dromedaries with two humps.

WILD BACTRIAN CAMEL

The first ancestors of all camels lived in North America more than 40 million years ago. About two million years ago, some types of camels left North America and went to Asia (A). All dromedaries and Bactrian camels living today are descended from these animals.

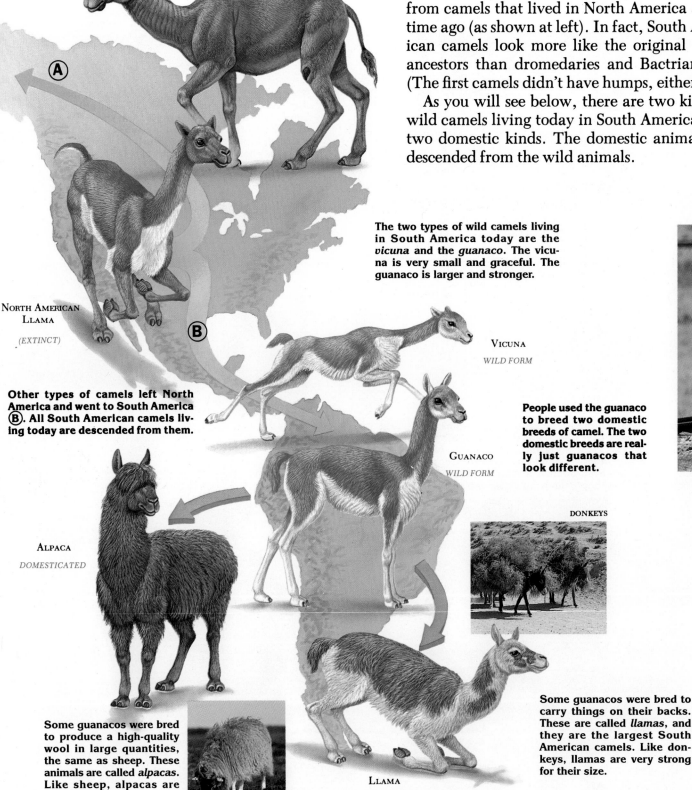

NORTH AMERICAN CAMEL

(EXTINCT)

South American camels don't look like dromedaries or Bactrian camels. They don't have humps. And they are much smaller. The average South American camel is only about *half* as tall as a dromedary.

But these animals are definitely camels. Like dromedaries and Bactrians, they are descended from camels that lived in North America a long time ago (as shown at left). In fact, South American camels look more like the original camel ancestors than dromedaries and Bactrians do. (The first camels didn't have humps, either.)

As you will see below, there are two kinds of wild camels living today in South America, and two domestic kinds. The domestic animals are descended from the wild animals.

(A)

NORTH AMERICAN
LLAMA

(EXTINCT)

The two types of wild camels living in South America today are the *vicuna* and the *guanaco*. The vicuna is very small and graceful. The guanaco is larger and stronger.

(B)

Other types of camels left North America and went to South America (B). All South American camels living today are descended from them.

VICUNA

WILD FORM

People used the guanaco to breed two domestic breeds of camel. The two domestic breeds are really just guanacos that look different.

GUANACO

WILD FORM

ALPACA

DOMESTICATED

DONKEYS

Some guanacos were bred to produce a high-quality wool in large quantities, the same as sheep. These animals are called *alpacas*. Like sheep, alpacas are sheared every year.

SHEEP

LLAMA

DOMESTICATED

Some guanacos were bred to carry things on their backs. These are called *llamas*, and they are the largest South American camels. Like donkeys, llamas are very strong for their size.

The wool of vicunas is the softest in the world. Hundreds of years ago, the Incas of Peru used vicuna wool to weave fine cloth. Only the emperor and his nobles were allowed to wear clothes made of this cloth. If anyone else did, they were put to death.

Llamas are still used as pack animals in the mountains of South America. Sure-footed and strong, they are perfect for the job. The largest llamas only weigh about 165 pounds, but they can carry loads that weigh up to 90 pounds.

To get wool for cloth, the Incas had a great vicuna roundup every four years. Yelling and waving their hands, they would drive thousands of vicunas into corrals. They didn't kill the animals. Instead, they sheared off their wool and let them go. In more recent times, people have killed vicunas to get their precious wool for luxury clothes, like the expensive coat shown at right. Now, it is against the law to kill a vicuna or to make a vicuna coat.

The future of dromedaries and Bactrian camels is tied to the future of nomads in Africa and Asia. As long as there are nomadic tribes wandering in the deserts and mountains, there will be camels with them, because the people will need the animals to help them survive.

But every year, the number of nomads in the world gets smaller. Thousands of them are giving up their wandering way of life and going to cities to look for work. This makes some people worry about the future of camels. There are still more than 14 million dromedaries and Bactrians in the world today. But how many will there be when most of the nomads are gone?

This is one reason why some scientists are trying to find a way that camels can live in the desert without nomads. They want to find out if camels can be raised like cattle on huge ranches. If this can be done, the number of camels in the world may actually *increase* in the future.

It is still too early to tell if the scientists will succeed. But even if they don't, it seems safe to say that domestic dromedaries and Bactrian camels will not become extinct. There may be